Exploring Food Chains and Food Webs

# POND
# FOOD CHAINS

## Katie Kawa

**PowerKiDS**
press

New York

Published in 2015 by The Rosen Publishing Group, Inc.
29 East 21st Street, New York, NY 10010

First Edition

Editor: Katie Kawa
Book Design: Reann Nye

Photo Credits: Cover tim elliott/Shutterstock.com; p. 5 (pond) Patricia Hofmeester/Shutterstock.com; pp. 5, 21 (fish) George Grall/National Geographic/Getty Images; pp. 5, 21 (algae) Ratikova/Shutterstock.com; pp. 5, 21 (tadpoles) ankiro/Shutterstock.com; p. 6 (both salamanders) Steve Byland/Shutterstock.com; p. 7 samarttiw/Shutterstock.com; p. 9 Janet J/Shutterstock.com; pp. 10, 21 (snail) Gts/Shutterstock.com; p. 11 Robert McGouey/All Canada Photos/Getty Images; p. 12 Guy J. Sagi/Shutterstock.com; p. 13 Gary Meszaros/Photo Researchers/Getty Images; p. 14 Erni/Shutterstock.com; p. 15 Member/Shutterstock.com; pp. 16, 21 (mushroom) Martin Fowler/Shutterstock.com; p. 17 Ruud Morijn Photographer/Shutterstock.com; p. 18 tmcphotos/Shutterstock.com; pp. 19, 21 (water bear) Roland Birke/Photolibrary/Getty Images; p. 21 (frog) Artur Synenko/Shutterstock.com; p. 21 (turtle) JamesChen/Shutterstock.com; p. 21 (bacteria) Nixx Photography/Shutterstock.com; p. 21 (pond) Pi-Lens/Shutterstock.com; p. 22 Dragon Images/Shutterstock.com.

Library of Congress Cataloging-in-Publication Data
Kawa, Katie., author.
Pond food chains / Katie Kawa.
     pages cm. — (Exploring food chains and food webs)
Includes index.
ISBN 978-1-4994-0203-2 (pbk.)
ISBN 978-1-4994-0204-9 (6 pack)
ISBN 978-1-4994-0202-5 (library binding)
1. Pond ecology—Juvenile literature. 2. Food chains (Ecology)—Juvenile literature. I. Title.
QH541.5.P63K37 2015
577.63'6—dc23
                          2014025935

Manufactured in the United States of America

CPSIA Compliance Information: Batch #CW15PK: For Further Information contact Rosen Publishing, New York, New York at 1-800-237-9932

# CONTENTS

# LIFE IN A POND

Many living things make their home in a pond. These living things are all parts of food chains. What's a food chain? It's a way to show the passing of **energy** from one living thing to another. Connecting two or more food chains together makes a food web.

Food chains are made up of **links**. Each time a plant or animal is eaten, energy is passed on, and another link is added to the food chain. All the plants and animals in a pond need energy to live and grow. They get it from the sun and other living things.

### Food Chain Fact

Plants get energy from the sun. Animals get energy by eating plants or other animals.

**TADPOLES**

**ALGAE**

**PUMPKINSEED SUNFISH**

This is an example of a pond food chain. The arrows show the flow of energy from one living thing to another.

# POND ADAPTATIONS

The plants and animals that live in a pond have **adapted** to life in this **habitat**. The water in a pond isn't very deep, and most ponds have a muddy bottom. Many animals, including frogs, turtles, and salamanders, bury themselves in the mud during the winter as they hibernate, or rest. Some animals, including fish and baby salamanders, have gills. Gills are body parts that allow animals to breathe underwater.

**adult salamander**

**baby salamander**

A baby salamander has gills that can be seen on its neck. Adult salamanders don't have gills. They lose them as they grow **lungs**.

Pond plants include water lilies, which float on the surface of a pond. They have wide, flat leaves to catch sunlight.

**Food Chain Fact**

Water lilies are known for their beautiful flowers, which have bright yellow centers.

# A LOOK AT ALGAE

Plants are the first link in a food chain. They use energy from the sun to produce their own food, which is why they're often called producers. Plants use the energy they take in to turn **carbon dioxide** and water into a kind of sugar they use for food. This **process** is called photosynthesis (foh-toh-SIHN-thuh-suhs).

Some of the most common producers in a pond habitat are algae. These simple producers aren't actually plants. However, they still produce their own food through photosynthesis. Many pond animals eat algae, which passes the sun's energy through the food chain from algae to animals.

Food chains in many kinds of water, including ponds and oceans, begin with algae because so few plants live underwater.

### Food Chain Fact

Algae provides much of Earth's oxygen, which is a gas animals need to live. Oxygen is produced through photosynthesis.

# POND PLANT EATERS

The second link in a food chain belongs to animals that eat plants and other producers, such as algae. Some animals eat only producers in a food chain. They're called herbivores. Snails are common herbivores in a pond habitat. They have rows of teeth that scrape algae off rocks and plants.

Beavers are pond herbivores, too. They use trees for food. Beavers eat tree bark as well as the roots and buds of other plants near the water. They also use the branches of trees that grow near a pond to build their homes, which are called lodges.

## Food Chain Fact

Some animals, such as salamanders, are mainly herbivores when they're babies. After they grow into adulthood, they become predators.

Herbivores in a pond habitat come in all sizes. Snails are some of the smallest animals in a pond habitat, and beavers are some of the largest!

# PREDATORS IN A POND

A pond habitat is home to many carnivores, or animals that eat other animals. Carnivores are the third link in a pond food chain. They could also be the fourth or even fifth link, because some carnivores eat other carnivores!

Many species, or kinds, of fish that live in ponds are carnivores. Many pond **insects** are carnivores, too. Dragonflies eat other insects, and dragonfly larvae eat tadpoles. When tadpoles grow up to become frogs, they get a chance to get back at dragonflies for hunting them. Frogs eat dragonflies, along with other insects, worms, and snails.

Adult frogs have also been known to eat tadpoles, and some bigger tadpoles eat smaller ones!

Dragonflies go from being a frog's predator to its **prey** as both creatures grow up.

# OMNIVORES AND SCAVENGERS

Some animals eat both producers and other animals. They're called omnivores, and they have many food sources to choose from in a pond. Turtles are omnivores commonly found in ponds. They eat fish, frogs, snails, and algae.

Turtles also eat dead animals in pond habitats. Animals that eat dead animals are called scavengers. Crayfish are another kind of pond scavenger. They have strong claws to help them catch live prey, but they also eat dead animals if live ones can't be found. Flatworms are also scavengers. They move along the bottom of a pond in search of food.

Turtles sometimes eat crayfish!

## Food Chain Fact

Crayfish also use their claws to **protect** themselves from predators.

# WHAT ARE DECOMPOSERS?

Food chains don't end when plants and animals die. Some living things get energy from breaking down dead plants and animals. These creatures are called decomposers. As a decomposer breaks down the parts of a dead plant or animal, **nutrients** are put back into the soil. Plants need these nutrients to grow and begin another food chain.

The two most common decomposers in a pond habitat are bacteria and fungi. Bacteria are so small human eyes can't see them. Examples of fungi include **molds** and **mushrooms**.

Decomposers have an important job in a pond food chain. They break down the bodies of things that die, allowing new food chains to begin.

# THE SMALLEST FOOD CHAINS

Entire food chains can be found in ponds that are made up of creatures too small for people to see with just their eyes. These tiny living things can only be viewed with the help of microscopes.

In this world of tiny creatures, the largest is the amoeba. An amoeba is only as big as a pinhead, and its body is made up of just one cell. Amoebas eat bacteria, algae, and dead plants and animals. A water bear is another tiny animal that lives in a pond. It looks like Earth's smallest bear, but it has eight legs!

A microscope is a tool that makes an object appear larger when a person looks through it.

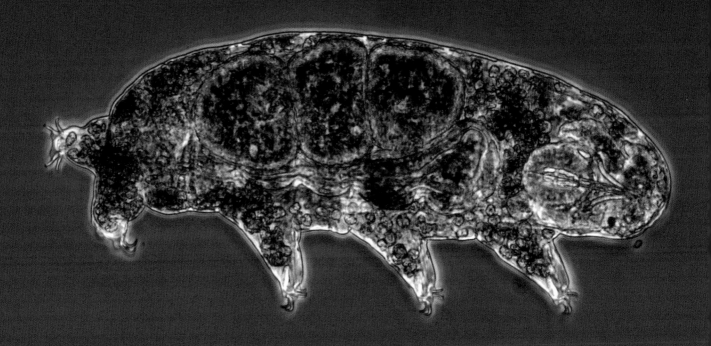

**Food Chain Fact**
Water bears suck
the juices out of
leaves and algae.

19

# A POND FOOD WEB

All the living things in a pond are connected. Those connections can be shown through a food web.

The colors used in this food web show the different types of living things in a pond. The arrows show the flow of energy from one living thing to another. The decomposers, shown at the bottom of the web, break down the body of each living thing after it dies, returning nutrients to the pond habitat.

## Food Web Key

- carnivore
- decomposer
- herbivore
- omnivore
- producer

## Food Chain Fact

Frogs don't eat the same things when they're tadpoles as they do when they're adults. That's why tadpoles and frogs make up seperate parts of a pond food web.

WATER BEAR

ALGAE

TADPOLES

SNAIL

TURTLE

PUMPKINSEED
SUNFISH

FROG

FUNGI

BACTERIA

# PROTECTING PONDS

The best way to learn about the food chains and food webs in a pond habitat is to visit one yourself. An adult should go with you when you visit a pond. Be careful not to hurt any of the living things in a pond.

People play a role in pond food chains, too. Pollution can make a pond too dirty for things to live in it. Building projects can take homes away from animals in a pond food chain. However, people can also work to protect ponds and the creatures that live in them. One way to do this is by keeping pond habitats clean.

### Food Chain Fact

Bring a magnifying glass to a pond to see the tiny creatures that live there. A magnifying glass makes things appear larger when you look through it.

# GLOSSARY

**adapt:** To change to fit new conditions.

**carbon dioxide:** A heavy, colorless gas that is in the air and is taken in by plants to be used during photosynthesis.

**cell:** One of the small units that are the building blocks of living things.

**energy:** The power or ability to be active.

**habitat:** The natural home for plants, animals, and other living things.

**insect:** A small animal with a body divided into three parts, three pairs of jointed legs, and commonly one or two pairs of wings.

**link:** A connecting piece.

**lung:** A body part in certain animals that allows them to breathe air.

**mold:** A growth of fungus that is often fuzzy and can be found on wet or dead matter.

**mushroom:** A fungus that grows aboveground and is known for its stem and cap.

**nutrient:** Something taken in by a plant or animal that helps it grow and stay healthy.

**prey:** An animal hunted by other animals for food.

**process:** A series of actions or changes.

**protect:** To keep safe.

# INDEX

# WEBSITES

Due to the changing nature of Internet links, PowerKids Press has developed
an online list of websites related to the subject of this book. This site is updated
regularly. Please use this link to access the list: www.powerkidslinks.com/fcfw/pfc